The Dark Moon
A Book of Poetry for Savasana

Tessa Marie Tovar

Copyright © 2018 Tessa Tovar
All rights reserved.

Illustrated by Megan C. Benedicktus
Edited by Cassandra Wick

DEDICATION

This is a book of poetry and soul searching. It is dedicated to my Grandmother Margaret Benedicktus, may she rest in peace and know that she is never forgotten. What she endured, and her family as a result, has had a ripple effect on my family, and in particular what I have chosen to do with my life. I intend to tell her story one day. For now, let this be a reminder to those that are struggling with mental health to seek help and know that you are not alone.

ACKNOWLEDGMENTS

When I put out my hands and asked to receive my calling, my life's dream and dharma... the answer was and still is writing. For many years I have put it off, believing the intrinsic and extrinsic voices that told me writing is a profession for the wounded, the miserable, the wretched drunk. No longer. With this book of poetry I now begin to share my soul, to heal through the path of the wounded warrior. To honor my ancestors, especially my grandmother. She inspires me from beyond the grave to be everything that she could not be.

Huge shout out to the support of my tribe, soul sisters, teachers and fellow practitioners along this path. Without you amazing women and men backing me up cheering me on and joining in the good work none of this would have been possible. Soul festers; Rosie Acosta, Kristina Coco-Hackenjos, Brenda Lynch, Molly Vance, Jessica Day, Michelle Thompson, Meg Dryer. Sister and Illustrator love of my life Megan C. Benedicktus. Best friend, editor, the woman who has seen me in my best and worst moments, bound by time immemorial regardless of where you are in the world (even though you moved to fucking Germany and I miss you like fucking crazy), Cassandra Wick. My parents David and Donna Benedicktus for teaching me to be free in body, mind and spirit. My husband Jorge Tovar for supporting me on this soul journey, thank you for doing the laundry and dishes so my hands don't get rashes. To my late grandma Margaret for inspiring from beyond the grave to write, write, write!!!

TABLE OF CONTENTS

THE KNOWING	8
SMILE	10
DARE TO COME ALIVE	12
THE PRACTICE	14
HOUSEHOLDER	16
AND SO IT IS	18
THE DARK MOON	20
A VERNACULAR FOR THE SOUL	22
LOVE IN THE FORM OF RELATIONSHIP	24
RIGHT AND LEFT	26
MISOGYNISTIC MYTHS	28
THE TRUTH OF IT	30
THE GOOD WORK	32
MEASURING SUCCESS	34
PURPOSEFUL TEARS	36
CHILDHOOD PRAYER	38
I AM	40
COMMITMENT	42
TRAUMA AND THE BODY	44
WHAT WOULD MAKE TODAY GREAT?	46
YOU ARE YOU	48
CHILDHOOD PLAY	50
FLYING: A THIRD PERSON PERSPECTIVE	52
NEW HEIGHTS: A FIRST PERSON PERSPECTIVE	54
LOVE LANGUAGE LANDSCAPE	56
MEDITATION MUSINGS	58
YOU'RE VERY WELCOME HERE	60
THE RIGHT WAY	62
STIRRING THE SHIT STEW	64
CO-DEPENDENCE	66

MOTHER EARTH	68
THE DANCE	70
THE MAJESTY OF ALL THERE IS	72
POST TEACHING GLOW	74
GRATEFUL	76
ETERNAL PARENTS	78
THE DEFINITION OF TANTRA	80
COLOR THERAPY	82
LOVER	84
WISE WOMAN WITHIN	86
GREAT SMOKING MIRROR	88
SPIRIT ANIMAL	90
KAPHIC KARMA	92
LESSON LEARNED	94
EYE CONTACT	96
DO YOU LOVE YOURSELF?	98
AND ANOTHER THING	100
EYES CLOSED	102
FATHER	104
MOTHER	106
SISTER	108

THE KNOWING

One day she knew
She could be silent no longer

She opened her mouth
A hoarse croak tumbled out

She stopped
Aghast

She clutched at her throat
The years of disuse and self-inflicted mental abuse had
taken their toll

She stood solid in her resolve
No more

She croaked, and squeaked, and got the jitters out.
Then after a time, and many moons worth of practice
A magical voice emerged from the depths of her shadows

People stopped to listen and stare at this wondrous site
The mute girl wasn't so mute at all
She had a story to share
One that all wanted to hear

She stood tall and began to shout
A loud booming lustrous voice rang out
The townspeople gathered about
Children and animals pushed past the adults
to revel in her glory

To share in the mystery of someone
Who had figured it all out

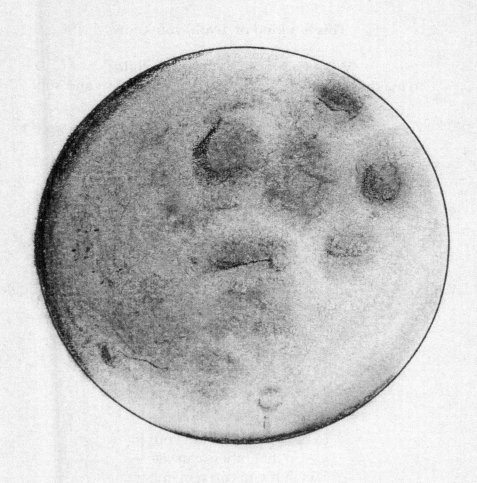

SMILE

She doesn't laugh much
She doesn't smile all that often
She has a rather stoic demeanour

This is a kind of death, you know

What happened to you dear child?
To make you lock away the gems of your heart and soul

The up-curl at the corners of your mouth
The twinkle and wrinkle at the edges of your eyes

Where did it go?
Why did it go?

Latent, yes
Gone forever, no

Would that I could, tickle you to bring about that innocent giggle
That unbridled joy
To see your smile light up your face

It is safe you know
It is safe for you here
In this place

To be happy to share your joy
So that others can see
So that you can remember

The bliss of this thrilling and terrifying life
It's worth it, it is worth the risk to smile
Again

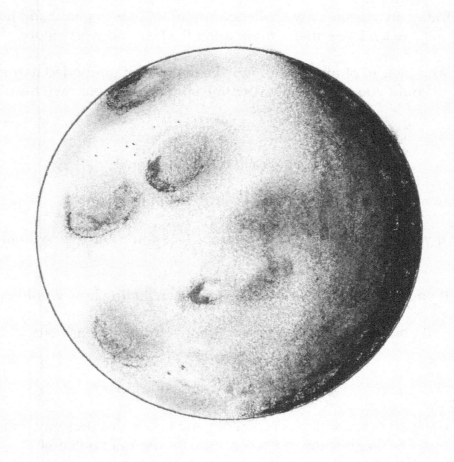

DARE TO COME ALIVE

What if today you woke up and told yourself:

Today my mission, my challenge, my practice is to pause and notice when I've gotten caught up in the fear and worry story.

And instead of unquestioningly believing that outmoded narrative could you begin to question the voice inside your own head?

Who are you?

Where did you come from?

Why do you speak to me in this way?

If you had to give the voice inside a face and a name who would it be?

If you had the liberty to choose your own ending how would it go?

If you had to make a guess at what your purpose is here, what would that be?

Can you answer these questions?

Can you practice the sacred pause and notice this present moment? No gripping, no expectation for a certain outcome.

Can you stay engaged without becoming attached?

Will you dare?

THE PRACTICE

The early morning dawn.

Duty calls.

A sacred space.

Breathe. Body. Being.

A milky pink cloud spreads out before me.

Eyes are closed.

A most gorgeous site.

Sparkling with delight.

The doorway has cracked.

A glimpse through time.

Beyond limits and the linear mind.

HOUSEHOLDER

Can I be a householder yogi?

The dharma of doing the dishes...

Maintaining an earthly relationship...

Sitting with the discomfort of unmet expectations...

Learning to set my own boundaries...

When do I say yes?

When do I say no?

When is enough, enough?

Those eyes stare back at me in the mirror...

Only you know my dear...

AND SO IT IS

Let it burn. Cast away this idea that:
You are not enough
You have no place in this world
Your presence is not valued
Because you are
Precious
Loved
Needed
Stronger than you know
No longer tell yourself that it is
Unsafe to be vulnerable
Unsafe to be emotional
Unsafe to be a woman
Unsafe to be a man
Or person
Or being
Adopt the new vernacular that you are
Fully born
Fully realized
Steeped and stewed to ripeness in all your power
You do belong
You have a gift waiting to be unearthed
To be appreciated, be loved, be cherished
By one
Or many
The quantity does not matter
The quality, the purpose, the why of the heart does.

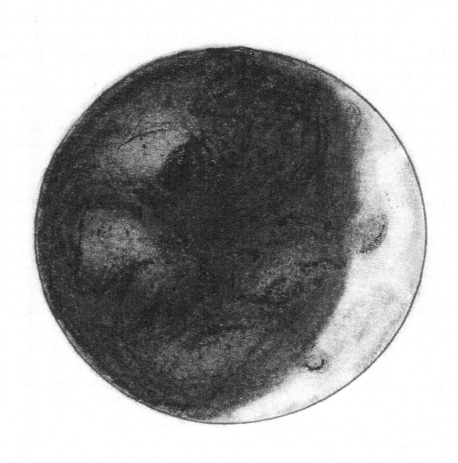

THE DARK MOON

A humbling practice as teacher and student.
A witnessing of other in awesome outward expression.
A realization of the art of word choice and placement.
An homage to the soul and spirit, calling for attention and acknowledgement.
A calling for the self to sink into, inward, in-on,
Its own awesome self.
What is shared out a reflection of that which is within.
A profound gratitude for feedback from the physical body, the house of soul, the vehicle of intentions.
The darkness before the light.
The winter solstice and new moon energy quieting the external pull of external needs, wishes, desires.
A time to rest into the quietude of dense dark matter.
An inward journey, a spiral of unknown.
Dawn not yet come.
A sleepy surrender.
A preparation for the awakening of the Full Moon on a New Year's day.
A celebration of life in its infinite cycle
Death-birth-growth-decay.
The lessons we need. There is no prescribed amount. That which is within follows without.
Vibration within, vibration without.
The sacred sound of A U M. Three letters personifying the layers of Earth, Sky, Air, past, present, future. "A" for dreaming, "U" for deep sleep, "M" for the state beyond and the silence that follows.

A VERNACULAR FOR THE SOUL

Illustrate
Articulate
Color in
Draw on
Explore into
Beyond a shallow depth
Invite your soul self to the party
The creative wild woman, man, person, being beyond gender
We all want to be acknowledged and seen; gift this to yourself.
Ask your sweet soul what she wants and needs.
The voice of ego smacks of should and shouldn't, judgment and
discrimination creating the illusion of other.
The soul self says I am that I am. I love you, I love you, I love you.
She said this to me beating her little fists on her chest
in the middle of a crowded restaurant.
Tears ran down my cheeks.

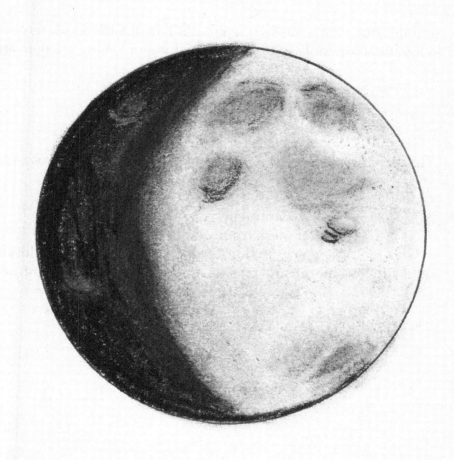

LOVE IN THE FORM OF RELATIONSHIP

Wounds surface in relationship.
Am I special enough for you? Funny question.

Actually, our hearts are so open that it has this tremendous capacity to love many people without diminishing or taking away from my love for you.

Anahata means un-struck.
The place where no darkness can enter.
No place for jealousy or greed.
This is not really love but rather the need or desire to possess the other.

I want to be your soul mate.
Let's let these fraudulent selves fall away.
Let's let these voices in our head pass by like floating clouds.
Let's you and me sit side by side and appreciate the magnitude of the heart.

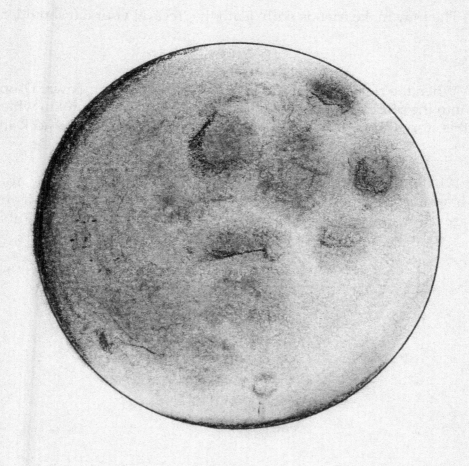

RIGHT AND LEFT

Hello right. They say this is my giving side.
Hello left. They say this is my receiving side.

They say make friends with death that rests at your left shoulder.

Notice.

When the right side is telling old stories. Write them down. Drop into the sense, the emotion and seek the place in the body in which this story is housed. Is it the heart? Is it the throat? Is it the neck and shoulders?

What of the left? She is quiet. You have to be still and patient. You have to coax her out of her hiding hole. She will come to you if you are ready. She will come to you when the moment is right. The ability to be still and receive her medicine is the sign of progress.

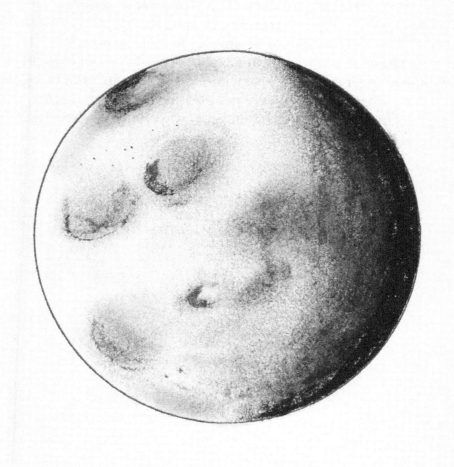

MISOGYNISTIC MYTHS

Household duties should come before self-care.
Having a daily self-care practice is selfish.
You are not enough.
You should be able to do it all by now.
I have to put myself in a box in order to be out of sight.
I have to meet everyone else where they are instead of recognizing that is okay to have people meet me where I am.
I don't have a voice that is heard valued or respected.

THE TRUTH OF IT

I have the right to take up space
I am a creative sacred being
I have the audacity to be bold to be seen to be heard
It is my birthright to be loved
It is my place to be spiritual and wonderfully weird
I trust myself
I make my decisions from a place of deep wisdom by listening to my intuition, not from my analytical headspace.
I can create a space for healing as my purpose suits without taking on others' suffering as my own.
If I take on others' suffering as my own, I am robbing them of their opportunity to ascend to a higher state of being.
I have the power to heal myself, in fact, I'm the only one who does.

THE GOOD WORK

The good work is met by resistance.
The voices of fear and judgment arrive to the party first.
The voice of wisdom and self-acceptance don't always have a vernacular, but rather rests in the stillness and silence.
Can I be with it all?
Can I sit with the discomfort?
Can I look at what comes up with a multifaceted lens of awareness.
The soft whisper of the belly breath soothing me back into my work.
Allowing resistance to be by my side, but not to take over as the conductor of this good work.

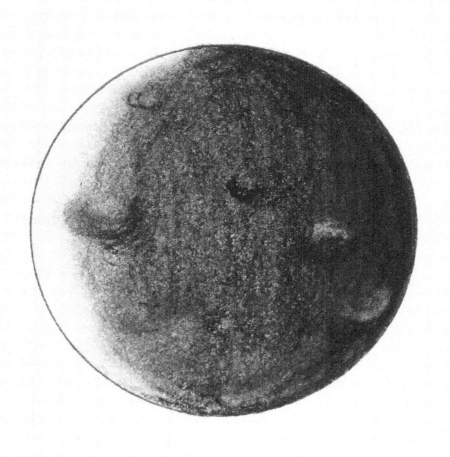

MEASURING SUCCESS

I ask myself;

How do I live a full and successful life?

What is my meter?

How do I measure my progress and success?

Can I allow myself to laugh fully, loudly, with eyes squeezed shut?

Can I allow myself to ponder the infinite wisdom of the universe and the intelligence of the human body.

Can I allow myself to be moved to tears by my emotions.
Happy or sad?

Can I do these things daily?

This is my barometer.

You might ask yourself these things too.

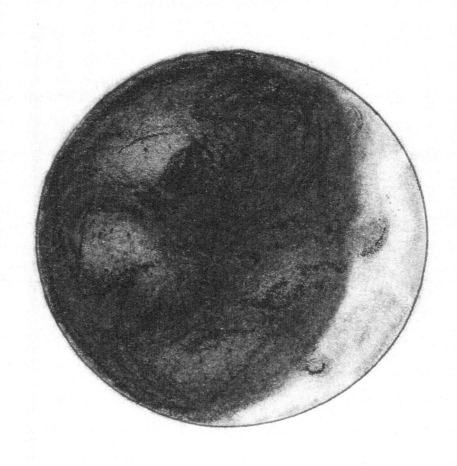

PURPOSEFUL TEARS

I started crying today.
Tears of gratitude.
One shape
One posture.
One simple rotation of the spine.
My body rang out the tears like a rag being twisted and squeezed after soaking up water.
It's always such a release when it finally comes.
A sense of bewilderment at why I've held myself so tightly wound follows.
Whenever they do finally come,
These tears,
It is cleansing, not unlike a bruise forming after being cupped during massage.
The tissue lifted so new oxygenated blood can flow through.
Clearing out scar tissue, unneeded, outmoded, knots and adhesions.

CHILDHOOD PRAYER

Establish your authentic experience. Make it your own. Sink into that.
Let that deep gut knowing guide you.
No second guessing. No hesitation.
Take the leap and find out what it takes to fly.
Spread your wings.
Feel the elements of wind and air, ruffle those beautifully unique feathers of yours. They are a gift.

This is your vehicle.
The only one you've got in this life. Treat it well. Let it do its divine job. To guide you, to keep you safe. To remind you that you will always be okay.

My mother and father taught me how to pray at a young age to Mother Earth, Father Sky, Grandfather Sun, Grandmother Moon. We said peace, Ho. Let it be. We smudged our sacred space.. We created an alter of sacred artifacts. We practiced the native American tradition of drum circles and sweat lodges and divine goddess worship. We honored the energy of the eagle and harnessed the harbinger of the owl. We always asked, prayed, in closing at the end for the reminder that we would remember that we will always be okay. We prayed for the health, happiness and help for those around us, our ancestors, our immediate family, our loved ones, our friends, all sentient beings.

May you remember that you will always be okay.
May you have help when you need it.
May you have happiness.
May you find a white light to guide you and keep you safe.

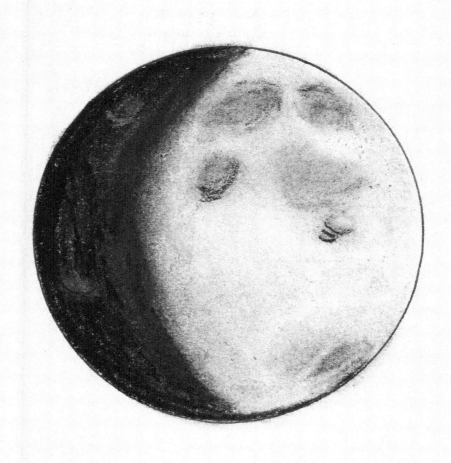

I AM

I am pure magic
I am love light.
I am fairy dust.
I am a goddess.
I am a high priestess.
I am, I am, I am, I am.
I am a healer with my word voice and touch.

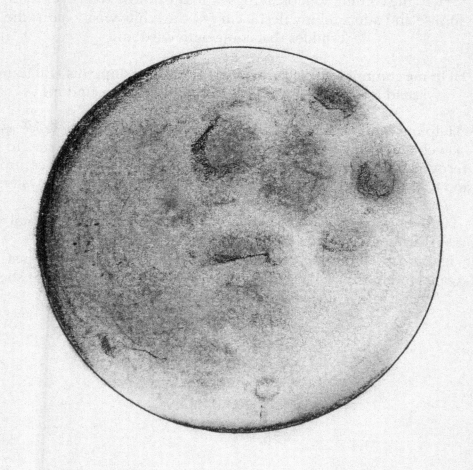

COMMITMENT

A prayer to the mother within
Help me commit to knowing myself deeply, all my tricks and trades
Help me commit to look at myself in the mirror with eyes that praise and adore all my fleshy curves, the white wispy hairs, the wrinkles that come with wisdom.

Help me commit to be true to myself in relationship, this will transcend into all facets of relationship to those around me.

Help me commit to truth in thought and deed, using my voice as a vehicle to serve up thoughts that are kind helpful and true. To recognize when I've gone beyond the borders of what I can control and to take a step back in awe of all that is part of the great mystery.

Help me commit to a deep knowing in the face of rejection. Stalwart in my truth and purpose and unshakeable by others' ignorance. Help me commit to friendship with the fear that just wants to protect me, she can sit alongside me for the ride, but she does not have license to drive.

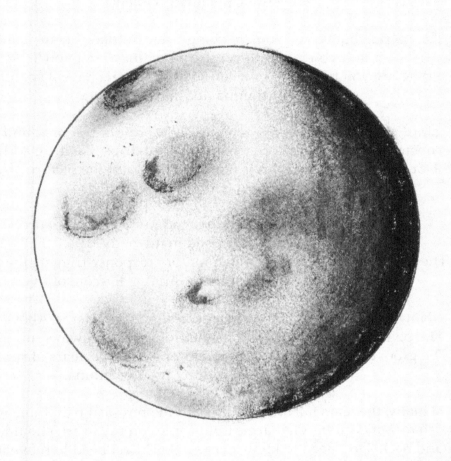

TRAUMA AND THE BODY

Leaning into the fear, the likelihood that it did in fact happen to me.
Forceful. Unwanted. Violent.

The patriarchal voice "you are being over-dramatic" rears its head.
Can't you just get over it. You're fine aren't you?
Who are you to complain when so many others have it so much worse. But trauma doesn't understand.

Unpredictable trauma triggers the flight or fight response and we constantly experience cortisol and adrenal drips like drug addicts. Don't misunderstand this is not meant to paint the picture of victimhood, but it does.

Beyond that I want to understand my own experience.
Where is it housed in my body.
The tissue remembers. The inflammatory response triggers the pain body. I languish in the science. An A.C.E. score of five.

Now how do I heal? I try to sneak around it. Under it. Above it.
The pain body is smarter and the neurological pathways run deep.
The grooves are etched thickly and after thirty five years of running they out pace me and my proud stamina.

Finally, the tears fall and underneath the physical pain I uncover shame and guilt. A lethargic thud settles on my heart, shoulders and neck. Do I need to know every detail? Do I need to relive it all and confront the aggressor? Where is my teacher that will lead me from darkness to lightness? I am alone in this, it seems.

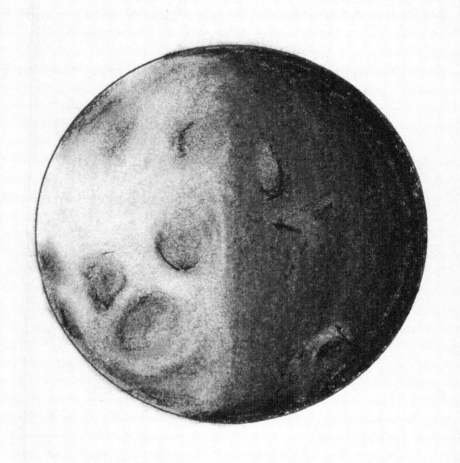

WHAT WOULD MAKE TODAY GREAT?

A relaxed easy going attitude.
An ability to look at challenges as interesting puzzles that can be solved. Approaching conversation and social interactions, both personal and professional, with a sense of curiosity, humility, light-heartedness and spacious awareness.

A realization that we are all beings worthy of love, who want to be seen heard and validated.

A practice in meditation.

A moment alone to breathe in silence.

A sense of connectivity with some force bigger than myself.

YOU ARE YOU

You may think you have no place to say this or that
It's possible that someone you love or someone you don't know will put you down, smash your dreams and hopes and tell you that is impossible.

The work is to continue anyway.
To recognize that is their own fear and that it has nothing to do with you.

Seek your solace from the moon shining brightly down upon you. Seek your solace from the sun warming your face and helping your flowers blossom. The universe does have your back and she wants you to succeed.

My teacher calls it being radically loved. I call it self-acceptance. My sister calls it Motherhood. My mother calls it dancing with wild abandon. My father calls it community service. Whatever vernacular you ascribe to, please make it your own.

There is no one else in this world with your unique flavor of goods. The world needs you to follow that bliss, to listen to that heart, to have the courage to open that door and see what mystery lies behind that pulsing gushy mash of gummy worms that sits inside your skull.

Remember there is no one particular formula that will suit us all. We may try on many other hats in this lifetime, but let your own be the one that fits out. That colors outside the edges of some prescribed lines. Perhaps that worked for them, but you are you.

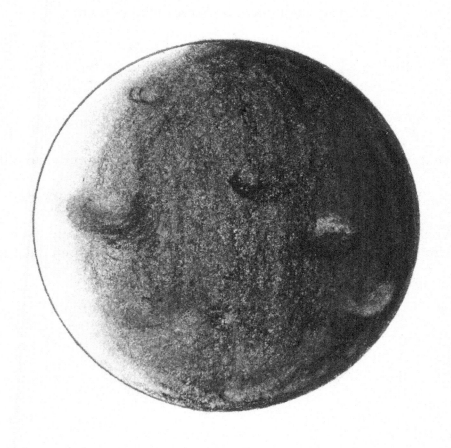

CHILDHOOD PLAY

A deep seated trust that I am on my own path.
A luminous meadow of green lustrous grass.
It grows just beyond that fence over there.

I want to frolic, roll and play.
Bringing back the days of troll dolls and Barbie towns.
Paving new roads and conquering evil troll kings.

And what superficial line holds me back now?

That imaginary wooden stake in the ground telling me as an adult
thou shalt not <fill in the blank>.
Take your pick I'm sure your own story narrative resonates.

What if you and I decided to take the lead and somersault over that
imaginary line to that soft blanket of fresh green carpeted earth.

Would you follow? Would it catch on?
Would we start a revolution? A reversal of time?
Back to childhood play.
Let's go find out…

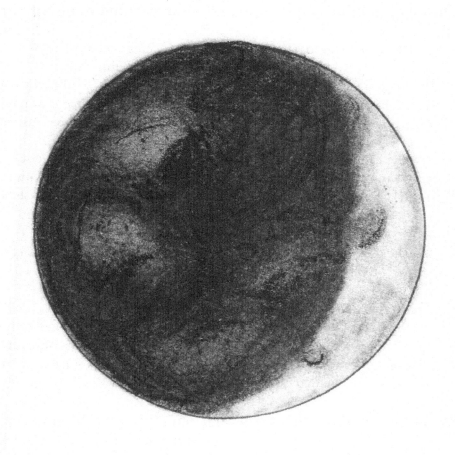

FLYING: A THIRD PERSON PERSPECTIVE

The dream realm gifted our girl with flight last night.
In keeping with past experiences she uses the power to escape a precarious situation.
Drudgery, trauma, pain and fear ensconced a sacred sleep body.
Recognizing the need to take flight.
The insatiable pull toward survival she prepares for take off in the usual manor. Running with concentration levity begins to course through her body creating porous cavity where there was once perceived denseness.

She begins to sore at first clunking along, a bird out of practice
Her wings disused for the past 20 years or so. She is familiar with the sensation as it lives in her reserve of what is possible with higher states of consciousness and worlds beyond the material and tangible.

As she ascends toward the clouds the trauma body loop is still active maintaining it's strangling grip on her physical body.

This world is not yet safe, she thinks, as she looks over her left shoulder. Death hovers there in the form of malicious men pursuing her and her fellow captives. She knows deep in her bones that freedom comes at the price of a journey inward, a trust in her same self body, spirit and mind which no other being can ever provide.

No matter how many nights, mornings, sunsets or lost moments she wishes for outward salvation.
Same self seeking will be the way into the love and the light.

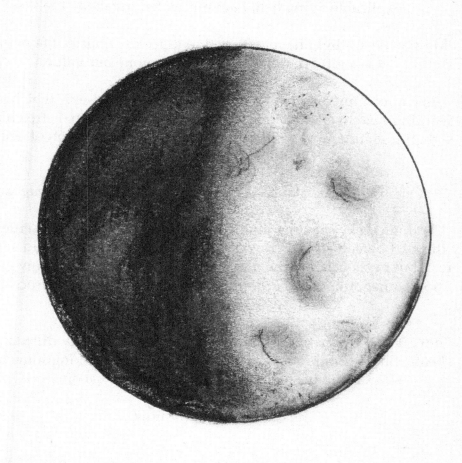

NEW HEIGHTS: A FIRST PERSON PERSPECTIVE

Spawned by inspiration to not only survive but escape some inexplicable living hell, I am motivated to take to the sky.

My powers of flight have returned to grace my quarter life period. It is a gift boundless of time and monetary value.

As I spread my ethereal wings, blind to the naked eye, which are working quite well despite several years of stagnation, I stretch and sigh. It is an utterance and ode to gratitude and sensation of being a completely whole being.

One backwards glance assures me I am approaching safety.

The domed sky caps my flight path at a new dimension. I settle on the next perceived level towards awakening. Technical, cold., austere, but my senses tell me it is safe for now. To rest. To let my intuition gather strength in order to receive the following instructions for forward motion and growth.

I am greeted by a woman ethereal. Wrapped in a lovely dusted rose sheath. She is luminescent, regal, resplendent in her kingdom of the sky. Cordially she invites me into her lair. I acquiesce.

It is safe enough for now…

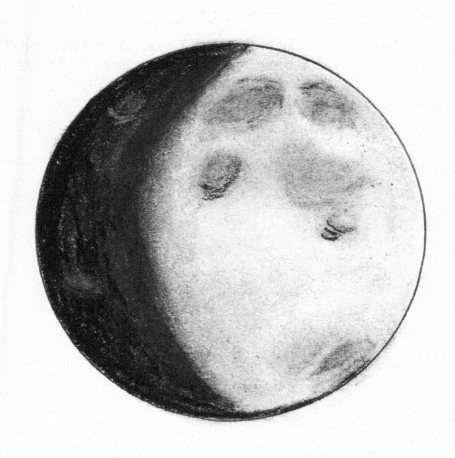

LOVE LANGUAGE LANDSCAPE

The landscape addressed only to the horizon in which the sun, as it sets and sails, kisses the place where the two meet for their serious date.

Then in no time at all the jealous lover of a moon shows its face looming above. Omniscient, the harbinger of the dark night of the soul.

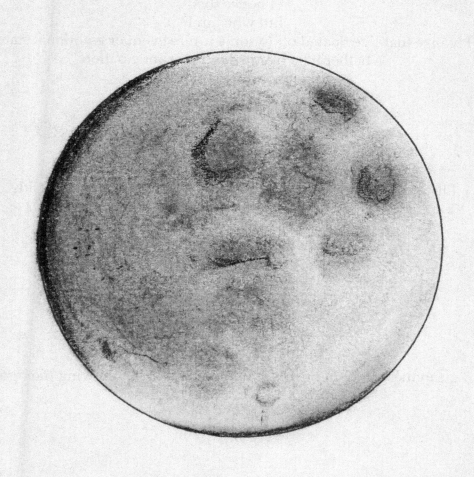

MEDITATION MUSINGS

Steeped in the practice.
The mind still wanders.
I notice this.
But who am I?
I realize that I've floated off to some future event or emotional state.
Whether it be planned or mere anticipation.
Premeditated pondering.
I notice this too?
But who is doing the noticing?
I bring it back into this room.
But what is it?
This particular space and time.
I listen to the pitter patter of the juicy rain drops falling outside.
I bring it back to this particular seat.
I notice the body aches and.
The tension in my upper back.
The desire to roll out my neck overtakes.
I begin to shift forward and then backward.
Recommitting to a steady seat.
Stillness, silence, peace and bliss.
It will come with time.
It will come with practice.
I glean these brief moments and know that I am following the right breadcrumbs home to the heart.

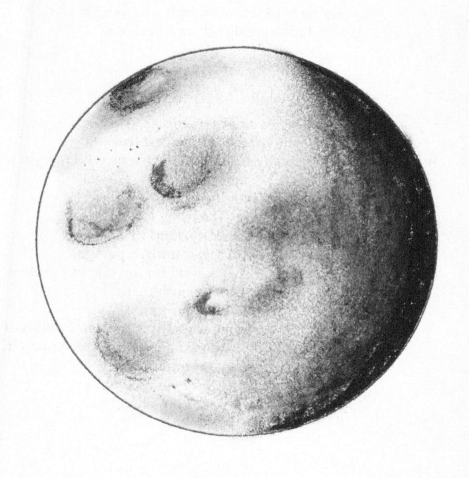

YOU'RE VERY WELCOME HERE

Here's the truth of it.
This is your life.
So you have to figure out what works for you.
I mean really go and find out.
Explore.
Try.
Test.
Taste.
Say yes sometimes.
Say no, to practice how that feels too.
Be sure to make the really important decisions with the gut sense
and heart.
Not the mind.
Ho! The irony.
Cliché as it sounds.
The truth is you are your own person.
Someone else's recipe may taste good for a while but pretty soon
you'll long for something new.
The next big fad or fix.
Then you'll get bored of the something new and different
And this is where and when you get to return to yourself.
It's magic and mundane.
All at once you come home to you.
You're very welcome here.

THE RIGHT WAY

Is it like this?
Should it be like that?
Which arm?
Which foot?
And where did you say you want me to put that?
Ummmm…..
Hmmmm…..
Why do I feel all hot and bothered?
Emotions rising form some craggy corner closet that I could have sworn I locked up nice and tight long ago.
Did she just perform witchcraft on me?
Did I just enter into a cult?
And now she wants me to make a guttural sound from my throat like some animal in heat?
No thanks.
Oh? It's optional?
Oh? It's all a choice?
Oh? I can go at my own pace?
Well humph she should have lead with that.

STIRRING THE SHIT STEW

The muck
The stench
The pain
The reverberation
The smear and stain.
The strain.
Grunt, growl, bear your teeth
Tap your chest and grumble through it.
Stir the shit stew
What comes up for you?

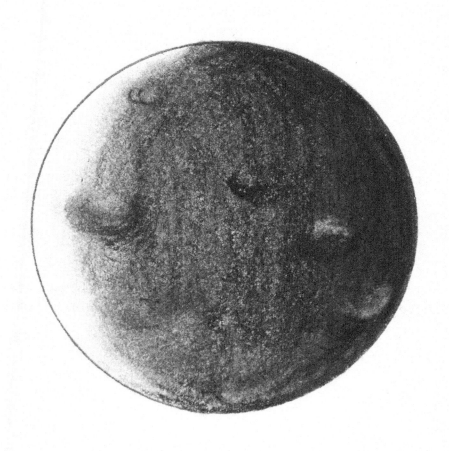

CO-DEPENDENCE

Evolutionary echo
Vibration matching
Inherited heart
Be small
Don't smile
Laugh on the inside
Grey face is your outward expression
You can make this person okay
You can get angry together
Be sad together

The lines between your feelings and my feelings disappear
completely

But what about unplugging from that habitual sucking and filling
of unconscious energy exchange.

How – is my question – when for at least 30 years of awareness
I have practiced to flinch into place at the demand of my soldier
saluting that it's time.

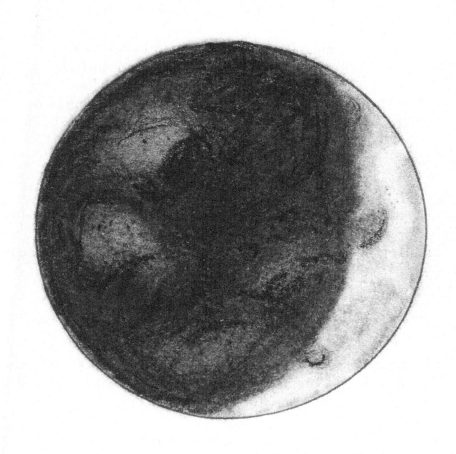

MOTHER EARTH

This is a story of my love affair with Mother Earth.
The great womb.

Lying flat with her, my heart to her rock.
Ear pressed against her smooth cool surface.
My heart beating in rhythm with hers.
Thumb drum echoing back into my inner chambers.
The sear of the hot water and minerals offered up by her,
from her craggy depths revitalize my skin
For now we are alone, she and I
The wild wilderness expansive in dimensions
beyond the naked eye,
The call of the birds, the rushing of the river in surround sound
She is my theater.
I look off to the blanketed clouds weaving in and out of tree tops.
She is so beautiful my breath catches.
I sigh in quiet awe taking in her majesty.

Lights on the horizon.
New beings are arriving.
Normally I would bristle at having to share her royal house.
But I let my breath carry me back to the realization that
separateness is an illusion.

We are all her children.
We are all brothers and sisters.
Hearts beating at dissimilar rhythms
And still disserving no less love.

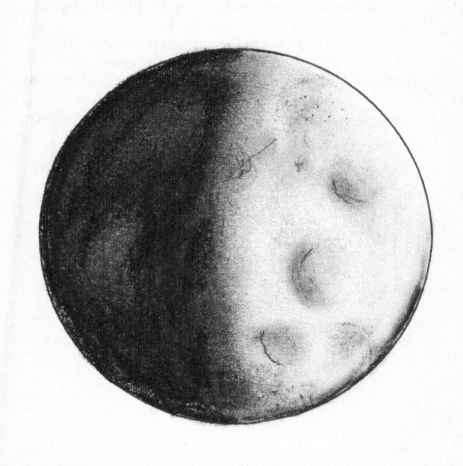

THE DANCE

Fully embodied and alive.
Moving my whole body to the rhythm of music.
Ear to ear smile.
Gliding north to south, east to west.
Flying, twisting and turning about.
Before I knew it two, three, then four hours had passed.
The dance floor began to empty out.
Still we swayed locked close in one another's embrace.

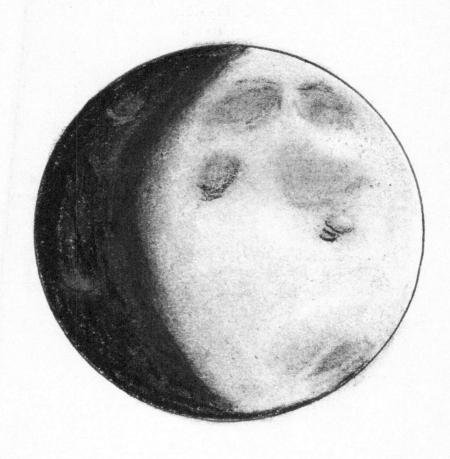

THE MAJESTY OF ALL THERE IS

This world is ethereal – it is – if you choose to see it that way
There is much more beyond the
Tangible
Touch
Taste
Sight
Sounds
Sit still and breathe
Breathe past your physical boundary
It is nothing but a mirage
A house to come home to, surely
But if we do not explore outside of our homely shell
Why, then, how will we ever come to know the majesty
Mystery
Magic
Of this deep vast multiverse
That is swirling all around us?

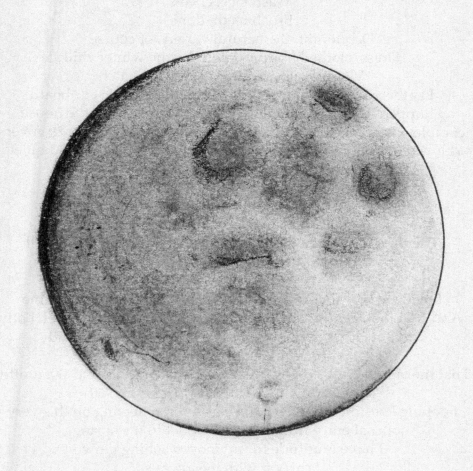

POST TEACHING GLOW

That day I awoke as usual before dawn.
I went through my routine:
Wash face, check
Brush teeth, done
Deodorant, the natural variety, of course
Dress, clothed appropriately for the winter chill
Vitamins, swallowed, down the hatch
I gathered a few choice snacks from the kitchen cupboard
I hopped in the car and slowly backed away from the house
complete with sleeping bodies still tucked under their cozy covers
I loved these mornings of darkness, stillness, all calm and quiet
I could see my breath in the winter air
Arriving at the studio to unlock, I am the first
Setting up in the usual fashion;
heat, low candle light, ambient music
The time for students to arrive; sleepy, dragging heals, still
half-dreaming came and went
No extra bodies arrived.
I realized that the student for that morning was actually me
And so, I took gentle care with placement of hands and feet, body
and breath. I decided to be my own best teacher and
find my practice on the mat.
That morning I realized how extremely challenging, and what utter
dedication it takes to show up for myself
Looking back on that day, two years later, reflecting on this very
journal entry from which the poet in me springs,
I have gratitude for my post teaching glow
I carry it with me always
It waits for those moments when the time is mine and mine alone
For the student in me to arrive, prepared and willing to receive

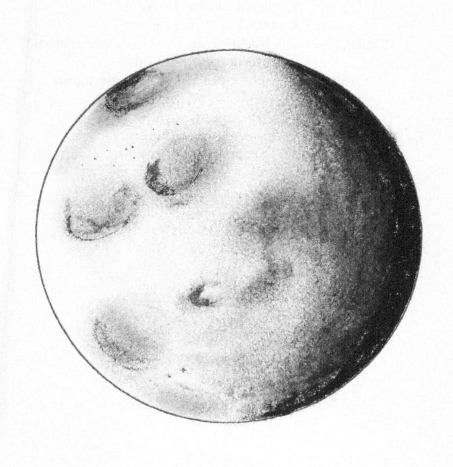

GRATEFUL

Grateful for this moment
Grateful for this breathe
Grateful for this practice
Grateful for this tradition and lineage of teachings
Grateful for all of you
Grateful for each opportunity to begin again

To try something new
To see something differently
To, each day, observe, arrive, and try again

ETERNAL PARENTS

Your physical form of a father has passed on
The divine form of your father lives on.
Mother Earth
Father Time
Always watching over you with a sublime eye
You are never alone
He and she are there guiding you, with outstretched palms holding your shoulders from behind
You need not worry, the physical body is temporary, ever changing
The cycle of life and death are ever present
The soul lives on
Stretching through eternity

THE DEFINITION OF TANTRA

Your eyes look concerned
Your eyes widen, expand
Your eyes narrow, contract
Your eyes soften, relaxed
We need it all you know

The expansive large reality of life
The awesome power of wind, rain, storm to sweep through
Shake loose the residual debris
A reminder that everything is finite, fragile
At the same time powerful and strong beyond belief

How many times have you sidestepped that homeless man selling
Street Roots in front of the store?
Averting your eyes asking him not to see the depths of your own
mess that you keep tidied away in a secret closet of the mind

Meanwhile homeless man is bare for all the world to see and we
judge him so openly
But really it is our inability to look at our own eyes in the mirror
with honesty, compassion and a willingness to learn

Grow and eventually expand beyond our own limited beliefs
That is Tantra to me

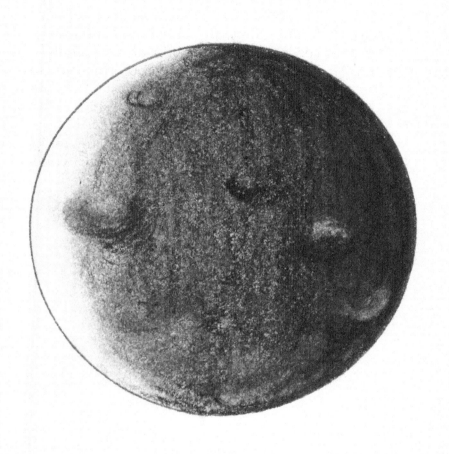

COLOR THERAPY

A journey through the chakras
They say that color is good for you
That a hue of red can invoke passion or rage
A touch of pink can invite compassion and love
A hint of yellow can insight cheer or melancholy
A dash of green is bound to the heart and brings you luck
A brush stroke of blue soothes,
calms and invites an air of introspection

A prism of purple can insight the deep knowing
A vision of violet will integrate the knowing that you are
the divine embodied

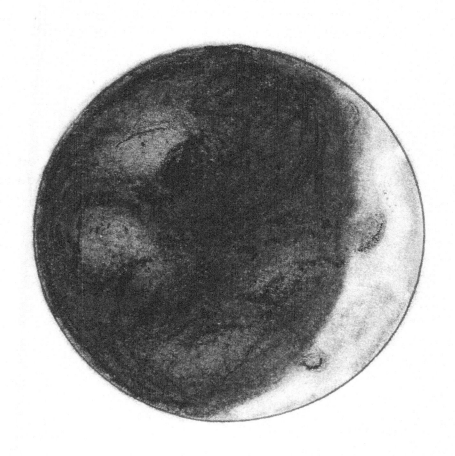

LOVER

Dear Lover,
My soul mate and one true heart's desire
Why have you been shy of me for most of my life?

Your silence stings
And yet when I speak to you
You speak back to me in riddles

The oracle truth saber of my soul
I have been counseled and coached into talking to you
even though your answers are vague and leave me wondering
To not foster this relationship with you would end in a
death akin to a cancer
A cancer of the throat, the heart, the intestines

For holding back my wishes hopes and dreams
I wonder can I speak to you and ever
feel a sense of peace or clarity?
I shall try and see

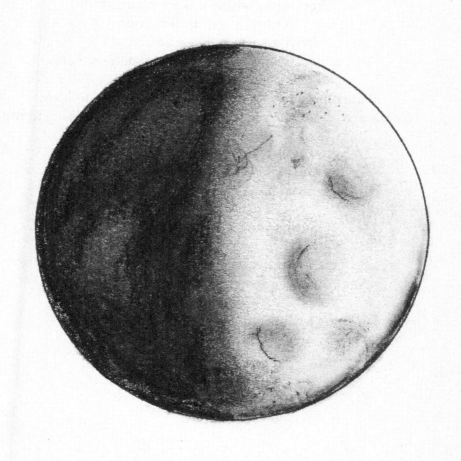

WISE WOMAN WITHIN

You came to me
Dressed in white, a silky silhouette
A glow surrounded you
Perhaps I witnessed your aura
You oozed wisdom, compassion, patience and
a seeking to understand
also confusion as to why it has taken me so long
to acknowledge that you have always been available to me

A billowy mist of sheer fog surrounded you
Our bodies edgeless borderless
You approaching me and I approaching you

You have been there all along
I see that now
You need no physical form
Yet you take pleasure in co-creation with me
My muse
My straight and steady arrow
My true north
My soul
My eternal essence

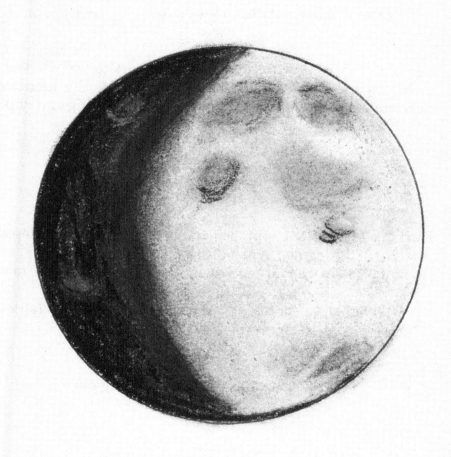

GREAT SMOKING MIRROR

The great smoking mirror
Is a reflection of your consciousness
Does it shine and gleam bright, winking back at you?
No?

Well then, you have some work to do
Newspaper and Windex was my father's favorite anecdote.
I would stand there spraying and wiping spraying and wiping
spraying and wiping
Until finally it shone

I smiled back at myself
Satisfied with a job well done

During adolescence I approached those little chores as a lesson to
be learned, a feat of strength to be gained,
a fantasy tale of a journey, adventure and intrigue to be retold

I would be transported into a world of gnomes and fairies,
fancies of flight and magic.
Warriors, princesses, queens, and trolls.

All from cleaning the great smoking mirror.

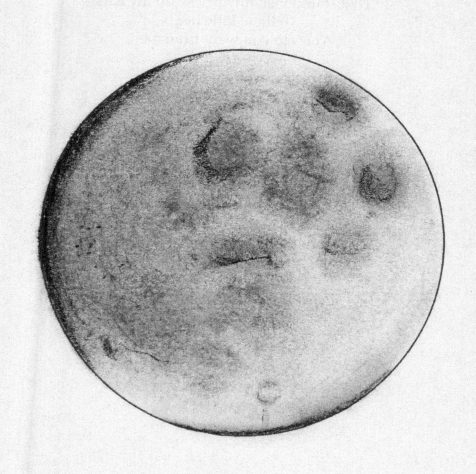

SPIRIT ANIMAL

They are attracted to me
Bzzzz bzzzz bzzzz bzzzz...
That sound instantly pricks up my ears
Tell me little bee
What do you want from me?

You deliver your venom
With a swift prick of the flesh
Then immediately hives break out and
I turn into an itchy, rashy mess
Once, twice, three times in a summer season
What is my lesson here?

Even in my dreams you visit me
I wake up in a sweat, heavy breathing,
hand grappling for my epi-pen
Yet you were not real this time

Still the torment ensues
I must pay attention to you

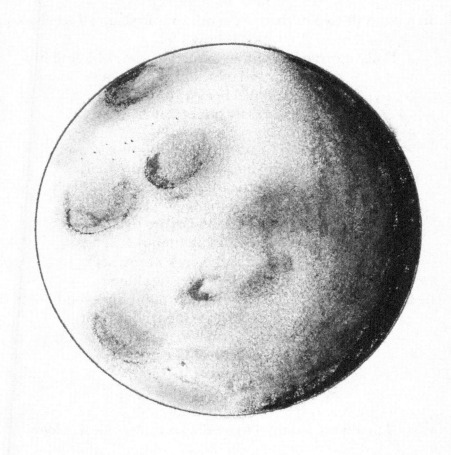

KAPHIC KARMA

Doubt, lethargy
Blah, bleh, blergh
In a word or two or three — despite ample sleep all week long —
this is how I feel
Daily morning meditations, acting and behaving in a
morally and ethically sound way
I still feel heavy, sluggish
Grossly out of touch

I worry that I have Grandmother's disease -
a predisposition towards depression
I feel like I'm doing everything as prescribed
Yet everything feels wrong
God I'm like fucking Eeyore over here
How do I break this spell
This tugging at the back of my neck
This weight on my shoulders
The little gnomes that have gathered around my eyelids with their
sole purpose to close them shut tight

I don't feel like it
Any of it
Showing up
Being kind
I just want to crawl in a hole and sleep, sleep, sleep

This is all too much
Perhaps I'm out of touch

LESSON LEARNED

Heart pounding
Neck ache
Sore wrist
Want to jump out of my skin

Fuck this
Fuck that
Aghhhhhhhhhhh

Why? What is this aggravating sensation?

Oh!!! Too much caffeine?!

Whoops -- try again tomorrow

In the meantime, there is my breath
There is my body
There is my heart

Everything in its place
And I get to lie right here in this sacred space.

EYE CONTACT

Standing across from one another
Ducklings in a row

We form two lines facing inward
Eye to eye
Toe to toe

It's hard not to blink
We are conditioned to look down

Bearing humiliation across our foreheads and hearts like a battle scar

Enough!

My sisters, hold your heads high
Walk proud
Let the tears come
Cry if you must
But be with us

A united front
We each are necessary
A piece of thread weaving the tapestry of life
Look at me!
Don't you see?
I'm your mirror
We all came from this same place

DO YOU LOVE YOURSELF?

She turned to me and slumped her
shoulders curved forward in a gesture of defeat
"I'm fat" she said and the corners of her mouth turned into a frown.

I looked back at her. A moment of silence passed.
At these moments I'm inadequate for a response.
I know what that feels like.
It doesn't matter how many compliments you receive,
the narrative has already taken the steering wheel.
You're on a wild ride of negative self speak.

What did I actually say? "Stop"
Looking back on it now I wish I had asked her

"Do you love yourself?"

What is going on in your soul, spirit, and heart to cause this
covering up of your radiance, truth and self-care?

Tell me your sorrows. Not because I have the wisdom to fix them.
But because upon divulging your secrets you may unearth a gem, a
truth so vital to the core of yourself that it shakes you awake."

You tell me quietly, half-hopeful "I'm here"

You are here.
You are trying.
That is enough.
Can you make peace with that?
Can you look into your eyes and see love reflected back at you?

AND ANOTHER THING

Remember that love is not jealous
But your ego is

The heart is vast, limitless, and expansive
The heart sees and understands all as vibrational brilliance

I know you just want to belong, to be cared for
Not disposed of

And that, my dear, begins with you
Accept and love yourself as worthy

These affairs that ego attaches itself to, they come and go,
dwindling out like a stubborn coal
left on the fire to smoulder on its own.

It's too fragile to grow or ignite without the presence of another
timber to keep it burning bright.

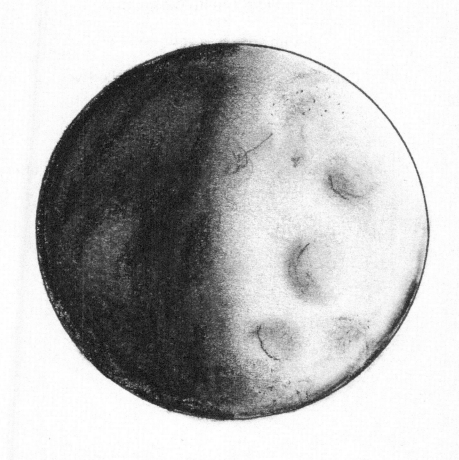

EYES CLOSED

Here's a challenge
Here's an invitation

Can you close your eyes?
And as you do
Can you begin to describe using adjectives

Descriptive verbiage only
No nouns

About all the wonders that the sense of sound has to offer

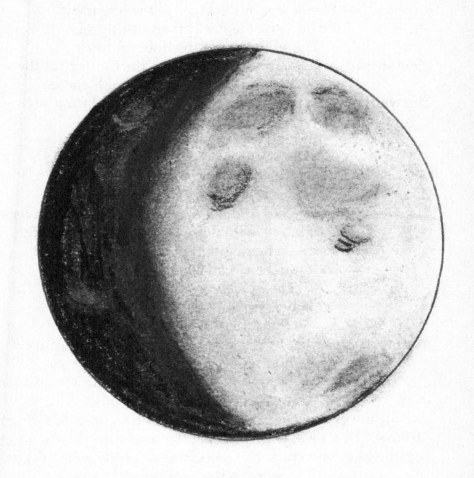

FATHER

She is a young girl
About 10 years old if memory serves
She descends the steps to the basement
This is where her Father's study sits
The silhouette of the door beckons
She steps across the threshold and into the mystery of the space
That he has created and that he holds sacred
The walls are papered with imagery, quotes, uplifting sayings and inspiration
Although to some it may feel cluttered
She knows to him every object has meaning
Everything carefully curated
He is soft at heart
He cries at commercials and tears up at the simplest conversation
His heart bursts with depth and reverence for life
He has given her a gift, it is in a way, she thinks,
an heirloom or inheritance
The exact word escapes her
A description tickles her tongue
She looks up at the quote
Well worn travelled by her roving eyes, day after day, week after week, month over month, year over year
She's combed through these lines looking for the answer
All the while thanking her Father
for the gift that she doesn't believe he realizes he's given
It says, "Don't ask yourself what the world needs, ask yourself what makes you come alive, because what the world needs, are people have come alive."
The gift is that he has allowed himself to be exactly who he is and in turn this gives her permission to discover who she is

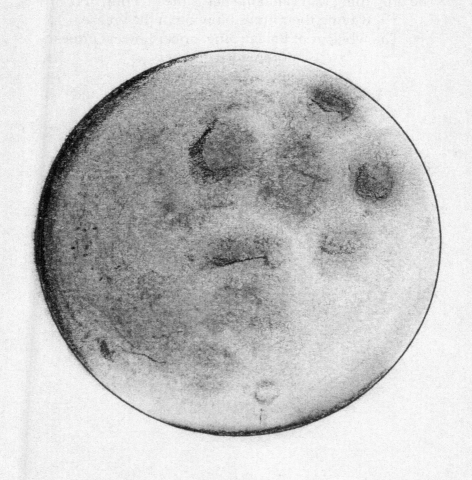

MOTHER

She is a fiercely independent woman
She lets the wind blow her where she pleases
The only thing that can tame her is the greeting of the trees,
waving their limbs blowing in the breeze
The whisper of the burning ember however does
nothing to calm her
It ignites a fire in her belly
When the music begins there is nothing and
no one that can stop her
She is fun loving and fancy-free
She will wipe that dance floor clean
She will put all you youngsters to shame at 70 years young
With all the charm, energy and whit of being 17

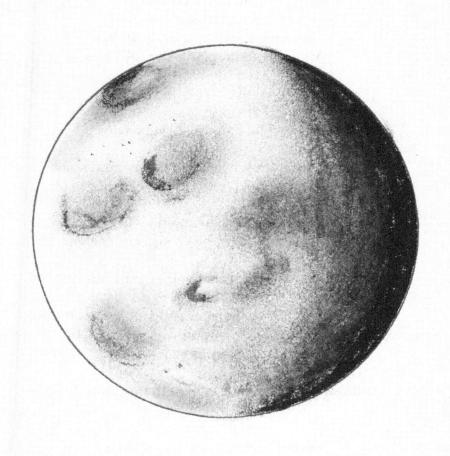

SISTER

Young at heart
Strawberry blonde
Small in stature
My little green sprout, I call her
My jolly green giant, she calls me
My little big sister

She and I are akin to night and day
Opposite in almost every way

Yet our love stretches beyond time and space
In any life I would know her face

Our Mother always wanted us to be close
Peace and love she would counsel

We would sneer at each other, curl our lips
Arguing as sisters do
I would sneak into her room and steal her clothes
Feigning innocence when something was returned but slightly out of place

And now, now I hold her here in this sacred space
In My heart
In my dreams
Sisterly love, as easy as it seems

ABOUT THE AUTHOR

Tessa is a Yoga Teacher, Health Coach, Writer, Podcaster, Reiki practitioner, Universal Life Church Minister, Lover of cats, Mystic and aspiring Witch (or perhaps a witch rediscovering herself in the form of modern day magic).

She lives in Vancouver, WA with her husband, her nephew, two black cats, and one black dog.

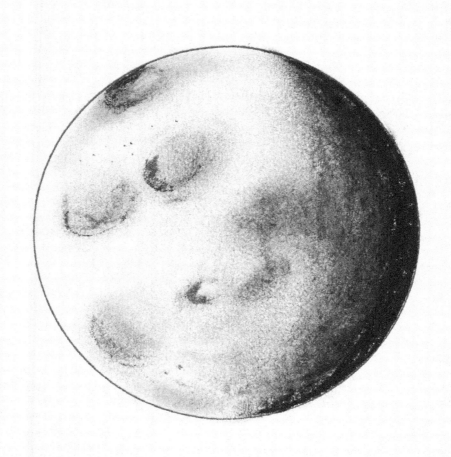

Made in the USA
Monee, IL
25 August 2019